I'M A BRAND

GAURAV GULATI

THANK YOU

Dear Lord,

First and foremost, I would like to thank Lord for giving me enough patience and the strength to write. I know, I can never complete and publish the book without your blessings.

Thank you so much for caring about me, guiding me and forgiving me countless time.

ACKNOWLEDGMENTS

First and foremost, I would like to thank my father Ripu Daman Gulati and mother Kamini Gulati for allowing me to realize my potential. All the support they provided me over the years is the most excellent gift anyone has ever given me.

I would like to thank my beautiful wife Ritika for supporting and keeping me motivated throughout this book.

Most importantly I would like to thank my late grandfather Hans Raj Gulati and late uncle JK Kharbanda for unconditional love, kindness and inspiration.

I would like to express my special thanks to Dr. AK Mandal for being such an awesome doctor.

ABOUT THE AUTHOR

Gaurav Gulati understands that in life, as in business, visibility is everything. As a personal branding & brand engagement consultant, he pushes boundaries and challenges limitations!

We're living in a tech-driven, interconnected world where personal brand and brand engagement go hand-in-hand. That's why he's dedicated himself to provide individuals and businesses with the strategies to future-proof their brands and boost engagement in this artificial intelligence world.

Gulati's signature brand building and brand engagement system encourages each client, from artists and models to entrepreneurs and politicians, to harness the power of their personal brand so they can work smarter, stretch farther and transform into thriving profitable monoliths. His innovative approach has been featured in various media reports and blogs and earned him the title of Asia's Leading Personal Branding & Engagement Consultant.

Gaurav Gulati holds an MBA in Marketing, PGD in International Management from University of the West of England and a BBA.HM. He has also studied Brand Management from the University of London and Personal Branding from the University of Virginia. As a Certified Six Sigma Black Belt Professional and Project Management Professional, he's got a unique insight into cross-industry trends and the cutting edge of brand positioning. Gulati's innovative approach is founded on the idea that in our fast-paced, increasingly digital age, everybody we meet has the potential to be a powerhouse influencer.

As a life observer, he regularly writes on business practices, management, brands and branding. His writing highlights real strategies to motivate and inspire.

When he isn't transforming lives through the power of personal branding and brand engagement he enjoys spending time with his German Shepard "Audi" and Rottweiler "Rochas" and exploring new food hangouts.

INTRODUCTION

Personal branding is a contemporary concept. Marketing initiatives have evolved over the years, and now, it has shifted to a new direction. The personal becomes universal. People are drawn to brands that tell a story a personal story.

I have discovered that personal branding is the outcome of the coming together of one's career, business, image, personality and behaviour (how you act and talk), and aligning these different areas with how the world perceives a person.

The self-perception and world perception should coincide with each other in order to create a compelling and relevant impact. It is about connections. We are lucky enough to be living in a new digital age where connectivity is much more accessible. The adage, "It's not just what you know, it's who you know." is more prevalent than ever. And as technology advances, being online has become the norm when it comes to communication; you must get on board with it, or you will be left behind. To grab a chance of achieving success means that your personal brand must stand out first!

The trick to creating a successful personal brand is authenticity. You need to be yourself and be seen as human, with interests outside of your work so that the people you want to work with are connected with you. Does this resonate with you?

So how do you understand who you want to connect with? And how do you go about doing it? Creating your personal brand is the key, but having the ability to reach out and connect with those who are just like you, or need you, or want to know what you have to offer is crucial. Let me help you get a head start!

1

WHY IS PERSONAL BRANDING ESSENTIAL?

Personal branding is a powerful and effective series of strategies that can transform how the public perceives you. If correctly applied, it can redefine your identity and make you more appealing. It can maximize your potential in order to attract new attention.

Personal Branding opens doors for you and creates an enduring impact on the public. By cultivating your brand, you'll have control over people 's initial perception. If you don't brand yourself, someone else will, and the consequence might not be in your support.

Relatively speaking, a strong brand influences its target audience and works overtime to engage those who may not have been targeted at all. A successful brand self-promotes, stimulates a unique experience, breathes loyalty, boost brand engagement and offers consistency in the quality of the service it offers.

The series of strategies work for traditional companies when it comes to their marketing efforts because this fresh take on branding attracts prospective customers and strengthens the connection with old ones. In the case of an individual entrepreneur or artist, model, or a working professional personal branding can help him or her establish a professional identity and showcase his/her competencies to the world, be it in the corporate one or in the community he/she is a member of.

Establishing a robust and relevant personal brand is not a mystery. It is the concept of combining various factors that catches people's attention such as attraction, message, authenticity, and execution. When we network, we have to follow an unwritten rule not to talk shop all the time. We have to build rapport first by discussing personal subjects such as hobbies and interests.

Studies have shown that consumers respond better to businesses, individuals and entrepreneurs who have social media platforms. The time when we needed to be formal in our interactions with prospective employers, business partners, and professional connections is a bygone era. In the age of social media, everyone is accessible even the CEOs of Fortune 500 companies.

Today, what you have to do in order to find excellent opportunities is to be different from all the rest. If you want to land an amazing job, then you have to create an outstanding resume. Get rid of the fluff and be authentic.

When you put yourself out there with a brand that reflects your personality, your core values and your social contributions, people will gravitate to you. One of those people could be your new boss or your new business partner or your new fans or followers. Take advantage of the tools that are within your reach. You have to dedicate your time and effort to establish a strong personal brand. It takes hard work, but you will reap the rewards for years to come. If you already have an identifiable online and offline presence, more doors will open, and it will be easier for the right people to find you. I will share some of the upsides of creating a personal brand that outshines the rest.

BOOST CONFIDENCE

Being fully aware of your strengths and weaknesses is an advantage especially when you develop your personal brand. Discovering which aspects of your life you excel in is a huge confidence booster. When you have a record of the things that you are good at, you have a better chance of creating a personal brand that people can believe in. Your credibility will soar if you know how to showcase the good side of your personality. A person who is self-aware can improve on his weaknesses and capitalize on his strengths, and the process of personal branding can help you do these essential things.

EVERYONE STARTS KNOWING YOU

Not everyone knows who you are, and considering that suggests they apparently have no idea what you do and how great you do it, it's essential for you to give your abilities a recognition. Personal Branding is not solely about you, but mainly about what kind of services you can offer. That means no matter who you are and what you do personal branding is for people of all ages and industries; artists, architects, authors, CEOs, managers, entrepreneurs, doctors, models, designers, lawyers, consultants, politicians and everyone from established Individual to fresher and professional to self-employed.

Every successful modern career is built on the common blocks of visibility, recognition, and professional positioning, the right personal branding establishes you as an industry leader, and help you stand apart from the competition.

ESTABLISHES CREDIBILTY

The one thing that matters most for any brand is credibility, and this holds true for personal brand as well after all people do business with people, not with the non-living brand. The best way for you to develop credibility is by being realistic and authentic in everything they do.

Credibility is about being consistent with your message; how you deliver it and how you execute it. As you establish your personal brand, people will see through your words and actions. They will know if you are being authentic or not. They want to believe that they can trust you. Following through with what you say to your target audience is the best way to go. To gain credibility, you should know what you're talking about and you should learn how to fulfil your brand promise.

BECOMING RELEVANT

Some of us want to change the world. Others wish to touch lives and become relevant to their community. A personal brand not only advances your career, it also puts your name on the map. You will be the first one in people's lists if they need help with an issue that you're an expert in. You become important in the eyes of your target audience and opportunities come knocking. That being said, you must remember that you can't completely please everyone. Stick to your target audience and show them that you can enrich their lives by being who you truly are.

SHOWS ORIGINALITY

Jumping on the bandwagon and following trends will not get you noticed. Showing your unique take on things is recommended for your personal brand to develop. You have to stand out and show everyone that you have something different to offer. Why would employers or clients hire someone who will share generic ideas and not contribute to the betterment of a company, business, or organization or client's needs? People are looking for something fresh and original. Embrace your out-of-the-box ideas and incorporate them into your personal brand. That's how you will shine!

IMPROVES FOCUS

In the process of creating your personal brand, you will soon discover your true goals and intentions. Naturally, as you move out of your comfort zone, you will be welcomed by several opportunities which you can say Yes or No to. When you have established a brand that has a consistent blueprint, you will no longer be led astray even when bombarded with new ideas. You will know which opportunities to prioritize and which ones to just let pass. If one option will not lead you in the right direction, you can just graciously disregard it. With a personal brand in the works, your focus is narrowed down to the bare essentials which are exactly what you need.

Building your personal brand from the ground up requires your full commitment. You should know how to market yourself effectively, efficiently, and successfully. The competition is tough; you have online and offline competitors who want to be noticed, too. If you tend to be just one of the sheep in the herd, then you have to change your game plan.

How can you stand out from the rest?

The trick is to get to know yourself a little better. Find out which of the things about your character are you most comfortable to share with the rest of the world. People are scared of releasing thoughts and opinions that they hold dear. What they don't realize is that their target audience appreciates honesty and they can relate to people who are truthful about their challenges. You have a social media profile which you can use to market your talents and skills. Having a social media account is an advantage because you can build your professional profile from there. Prospective employers may take a look at your Facebook or Instagram or LinkedIn profiles so you have to make sure that you fill those profiles with content that shows your potentials and your character.

What is your unique selling point? That's one question that I can help you discover through this book. If you stick with me, I'm going to show you how to explore your natural gifts and talents. But not just yet! You will need some time and space for that so for now, it's important for you to understand why you should have a powerful personal brand both online and offline.

A personal brand is about defining your own image, the one the world perceives you to be. When you are successful at this, you will appeal to a wider audience and rise as a winner in your field of endeavour.

Pay attention to the businesses that thrive in their own respective industries. What do they have in common? Their customer service is top-notch. Their interaction with their clients and customers is amiable, helpful, and seem to always benefit the people they are trying to serve. Customers gravitate to stores, brands, and businesses that know how to take care of them. They see a positive attitude as a signal that a brand wants to give them only the best. A great first impression goes a long way.

How do we create a personal brand that is relevant to your target audience? How can we capture their attention and let them believe that you have their best interest at heart? One effective way to go about this is to portray yourself as an authority in the field. You share relevant and helpful blogs, articles, and videos that inform, educate and entertain them. By doing so, they will consider you as someone they can turn to when they need advice about a certain product or service.

It is not enough that you have formulated your personal brand; you also have to create an effective marketing strategy that utilizes all the tools that exist within your reach. Is your face and voice charming and powerful? You can make an impact by showing what's behind the brand, and that is the person behind the product or service. Now, you have to plan your marketing initiatives and make sure that everything goes according to plan for the duration of a year. Then you have to evaluate if your marketing plan is on track and change course if necessary.

Plan your personal brand well. This means no details should be overlooked. The simple act of creating a winning elevator pitch that will get people hooked right away is already the first step at the door. This little detail is necessary to establish your offline presence. Telling people what your brand is about and what value it can provide them within a minute is a feat in itself. You have just grabbed their attention. What's the next step?

2

DISCOVER YOUR NICHE

The most crucial part of creating a personal brand is to find exactly who you are. Discover your character through the eyes of others. What do they like about you? What do they dislike about you? After you find out exactly who you are and what others like and dislike about you, then the time is ripe to bring out the best version of yourself for the world to see. Your perception of your brand is limited. You need the help of others to determine if what's in your mind is consistent to what they think. Let them collaborate on shaping your brand image, only then can you project your unique brand identity. The result will be positive for your career and for the people you want to help or connect with.

As challenging as creating a brand from scratch may seem, you shouldn't be discouraged. Think of the fruitful outcome of all your hard work. When people know exactly what your brand stands for, you will have more loyal customers, and more people would want to invest in you and help you grow.

Successful branding is not a one-size-fits-all formula. Some brands have the X factor while others are just generic. What great marketing can help you do is give your brand the right exposure. In business, you may have the best product, but if you don't know how to market and sell it, then you lose. It is similar to personal branding; if you don't put your brand in the right online or offline platform, you risk being seen as one of them. You don't stand out at all. You have to ask the question, "What motivates people to respond to your brand positively?"

Opting for one brand over the other seems to suggest that one is better than the other, but you have to keep in mind that people's perceptions are subjective. Hence, you have to find out about how people make their choice. What triggers them? This is where experience comes in. What kind of situation was the buyer in when he was shopping? Did your brand solve his problem or gave him the solution he was looking for? Customer experience is important. His interaction with your brand is crucial to determine if he will like it or not.

Has your brand built an instant connection with your customer? That connection can be strengthened with the right strategy. When customers relate to your brand, it will be easier to draw them in the marketing funnel and guide them to what you want them to do. It's a two-way street. On the one hand, you attract them and tell them you have something of value that they can benefit from and on the other; they will contact you, buy from you, and do business with you. Brand Engagement Transpires; ultimately you are creating a bond or a relationship with your target market/audience.

If you have a common ground to build a foundation on, then the relationship naturally evolves. More common interests mean more opportunities to communicate in the future. This is vital in the personal branding process. You can connect with your customers and the feedback that they give you can be an essential tool for enhancing your brand. As you develop your brand, your target audience gets to see your other layers, and they will feel more attuned to the message that you convey.

It would seem as if you are working together with your patrons.

Sincerity is important. Don't think that the people you serve can't see past your mask. You have to take the mask off and reveal endearing qualities about your personality. This is where your brand really connects with your audience, and brand engagement occurs. Stay focused and don't dabble in other areas that you are not an expert in. People would not respect a fickle-minded person. Stick to the goals you want to achieve and your customers will notice your consistency.

I have designed this book to help you build a brand that is entirely and uniquely yours. These fundamental concepts will be your guiding light in creating a consistent and concise brand. Every essential detail that you need to know is incorporated in these 5 fundamental concepts:

1. DEFINE YOUR PERSONALITY

One personality is attractive to a set of people while another personality can please another group. For example, if you are an introvert, most likely people who also exhibit those traits can relate better to you compared to extroverts. Introverts will identify with you, share your passions, and believe that what you tell them is the truth. The key to capturing the right audience is to identify your brand personality in the beginning. Your brand will be engaging to your audience if it is more specific and caters to them especially. When you have identified the dominant traits in your personality – your strengths – you can put the focus on them so that people who have similar qualities will connect with you. They will engage with your brand.

Have you noticed that people with the same character such as being friendly, charming, and kind flock together? They share the same values hence it is easier to group them together. When you broach a certain topic, the conversation seems to be flowing because the people in this group agree with each other. You recognize yourself in the each of the person in the group. Proposing a business idea will be much easier and there is a bigger chance of it being supported rather than if you shared it with a greedy person. When it comes to your brand personality, you have to be extra cautious because no one wants a fake. If you are being authentic, people who share your personality are more likely to patronize your brand or help you with your goals.

2. OWN YOUR STRENGHTS

Once you figure out your unique personality, you have to explore the part of yourself that excels at one or two things. What area are you good at? Are you better than anyone else you know in this area? By highlighting your strengths in a certain field, you solidify the originality of your brand. You possess a rare quality which you can capitalize on by transforming that into your very own niche. It could be architecture, finance, self-help, or any other passion that you are pursuing in your life. When you have that in the bag, it will be easier to focus your energies on planning the marketing efforts that cater to your niche market.

Having your own niche allows your personal brand to expand and be known for your identifiable qualities. You distinguish yourself from the rest so that your brand can be in the spotlight.

3. DETERMINE YOUR PURPOSE

Life is not all about what you do or about making money. You will discover that you cannot sustain your career, your relationship, or your business without a clear direction on the horizon. After knowing yourself and discovering your unique selling point, the third concept is a bit closer to the heart. You have to determine your purpose. Why are you doing what you do? When you take the money out of the equation, will you still be happy with the work that you do? Will you feel as if you are fulfilling your promise to the world with the kind of path that you chose? These are loaded questions that when answered can give you a concrete idea of your key motivation. In company profiles, they call this a mission statement. For your personal branding journey, you can call this a brand promise.

Personal branding is about creating and nurturing connections with your target audience. When you fulfil a brand promise, you are satisfying their needs and they become happier with their interaction with you. With this kind of progress, you are getting closer and closer to achieving your goals.

4. AWARENESS OF THE COMPETITION

There are billions of people on the planet and chances are high that you will find ideas similar to yours permeating everywhere. You will have to compete with others to catch the attention of the same group of people, your shared target market. It's going to be tough and you have to be ready for that.

A life coach who has written a book that caters to professionals can see another life coach who has done a similar endeavor as a competitor. Their offerings should be further differentiated from each other by narrowing down the target market even further. For example, you can divide your target group into three namely, young professionals, women, and journalism. Your book will only appeal to the group you specified which eliminates many of your competition in a broad spectrum.

Observe and study your competitors closely. Discover what makes them successful or what made their businesses fail. You learn from both the successes and the failures of others especially your competition. You are moving in the same circle and you can glean from the feedback of their customers in order to improve your own products or services. Have a look at their marketing initiatives and see if they connect with the audience effectively. You have the power to transform this gathered knowledge into your own weapon.

5. SPECIFY YOUR TARGET

Your target market is a group of people who resonate with who you are. They want what you have to offer but they need to be convinced of its worth. You have to strengthen your connection by treating them as you would treat yourself. As a person, you have layers within you. The sum of your personality is divided into categories such as your career, relationships, economic status, hobbies, and interests. By understanding these aspects, you will be able to group your target audience into different categories as well and these are:

- Lifestyle: conservative, exciting, trendy, economical
- Social Class: lower, middle, upper
- Opinion: easily led or opinionated
- Activities and interest: sports, physical fitness, shopping, books, movies
- Attitudes and beliefs: environmentalist, security conscious, religious

By dividing these different aspects, you will have a better understanding of your target audience and what you can offer in order to please them.

When it comes to your personal brand, your reputation is a vital piece of the puzzle. In your social and professional circle, having a good reputation can be the difference between a closed business deal and a renewed relationship. If people perceive you as honorable and trustworthy, it becomes automatic that they trust your brand as well.

Going the extra mile to fulfil the needs of your customers and clients can boost your reputation. If you own a company that renders services then your customers are expecting that you would go above and beyond to please them. If your crew over-delivers, this positive quality reflects on your brand. Each and every detail in your company plays a role in showcasing your brand and what you're all about. Hence, it's important to cultivate a company culture that's healthy, helpful and respectful of staff, colleagues and customers.

Let me make it clear. Personal branding is not about what's on the surface. People can see what's on the exterior but they care more about what's inside that's why your brand has to be consistent. From packaging, promotions, delivery, to the actual product itself, everything should be exactly what your brand promised. The customer service experience of your clients should also be taken seriously. All these factors combined can boost the reputation of your brand.

Keep in mind that your personal brand will be long-lasting thus you have to create a great first impression and sustain that for as long as it is necessary. Huge brands such as Nike, American Express, and McDonald's take care of their reputation. They have established it for several decades; they will not do anything to jeopardize what they have built. You will benefit greatly if you follow in their footsteps.

3

CREATE A UNIQUE PERSONAL BRAND

Branding is not just for companies and large businesses. Nowadays, creating a personal brand is advantageous to your own career development. Most of us who have discovered this secret is no longer wracking their brains on how to improve their resumes to make them noticeable. They have a new strategy to get employers, clients and opportunities to find them. You can make your own unique personal brand by starting with your social media profile or starting a blog. The difference with this method from the traditional ways of looking for jobs is that you are showing your proactive and driven side. You are not waiting for a call. You are putting yourself out there so employers/clients/opportunities will be drawn to you.

Imagine heads of HR reading through hundreds of resumes during the day and being frustrated about not finding the perfect candidate. They are not going to sit in their office chair and wait for the right person to come along in this day and age. They will look for alternative platforms in order to find talented, creative, assertive, and driven individuals. These are the people they are looking for. They want people who have the initiative to take on the challenge of marketing themselves. They prefer people who they don't have to monitor every single time but who are self-reliant and courageous. By creating your personal brand, you are showing everybody that you can do the job even if you are not hired yet. You are exhibiting leadership skills early on.

Having a personal brand is similar to defining your goals, and employers - clients who are “doers” are attracted to that kind of energy. They are seeking individuals who have a plan. When you have started formulating a brand, you will discover so many pros and cons of your decisions. You will uncover your strengths and limitations which will enable you to compensate for whatever it is that you lack in the skills department. Carefully studying what employers or clients in your field are looking for and matching those qualities with the ones that you possess makes your opportunity hunting more systematic.

Embrace this great opportunity of discovering your excellent skills and talents. You have a good reason to ask your loved ones, friends, and former colleagues for feedback and listen to their advice on how to improve yourself. The time is ripe to open this type of conversation with people who are aware of your weaknesses. They will help you see the light so that when you present your brand, you will have people you trust to support you and put you back on the right track if you are astray.

Once you have decided on the type of brand that’s perfect for you, make sure everything you do fits that brand. Your actions, projects, goals, clothing, personality, and lifestyle must suit the brand you have designed for yourself. Armed with the tools of technology today, you have the ability to transform your work life and your personal life. You can project these changes on your social media platforms. Furthermore, I recommend that you be constantly present on social media and your postings must match your personal brand. Carefully thought out and interesting posts on Facebook or Instagram can endear you to your target audience. Try to review your account settings to avoid any involuntary photo tagging being viewed by potential stakeholders that may not be aligned with the personal brand image you are aiming to project.

Employers are using social media more and more in their search for new employees. Everything you post can affect your appeal to the people who may want to hire people in your field. Your social media profile can be the difference between getting an interview or being overlooked during the early stage of the interview process.

Exerting effort in building a brand image and consistently living up to the level of authenticity that you have committed to will provide the opportunity to advance your career and open up incredible opportunities.

Seeing yourself as a product that you should improve and market is one effective way of looking at it. You can manage what is recognizable about yourself and incorporate it into your brand. How do your peers, colleagues, suppliers, customers, friends, and clients see you in the areas where they interact with you? Can you describe your personal impact on people? Adjectives such as cooperative, generous, fair, and approachable can be indicative that the person described is a great leader. Do you believe that you possess the qualities of a good leader? Your LinkedIn profile can reflect your track record, accomplishments and even your professional relationships.

Today, we are influenced by what we see visually. People are even too lazy to read books nowadays, and we respond more to images and infographics. The practical way in which you can tweak your visual perception is through your clothing style. You should look the part when you're in a meeting or joining an important event. The next part that you should look into is how you communicate through words and actions. Do you know that your body language sends a signal to the person that you encounter? Mirroring the actions of the person you're speaking with makes him feel at ease in your presence. Your tone of voice, your smile, and the way you carry yourself ultimately add up to your entire existence. Make sure that each interaction with a client, customer, or stakeholder leaves a positive impact.

Your heightened self-awareness can be your secret weapon in ensuring that your brand image is exactly congruent to your authentic self. When you do something inconsistent, you have the power to revert back to words and actions that reflect your personal brand. For example, you have a business that promises to deliver on time so every time you have a meeting, you always have to show up on time, too. People will think that the owner of the business walks the talk and you have plus points for that. In the planning stage of your personal branding, feel free to write down what your brand should project so that you can remind yourself of all these pointers as your brand grows over the years.

First impressions are crucial, and you have to nail them down before anything else. It's important that you ask yourself these questions:

- How do you want people to feel when you enter a room?
- How do people perceive you in your first meeting?
- How can you break the ice effectively?
- What topics should you discuss to keep the conversation flowing?
- What kind of ideas do you want to share before you leave?

In your personal branding, it is natural that you define yourself, your character, your work ethic, and how you deal with people.

Are these themes similar to your behaviour? When you claim that you're in control, can you face stressful situations?

Now, your image must be authentic. Your physical appearance should reflect a part of your personality. I'm talking about clothing choices. You appear professional on your LinkedIn profile, but you wear shabby clothes when you're in public. The connection is lost. You have to be consistent. In meetings with clients, you have to wear casual yet professional clothing if that is your style. You can't suit up if you're the type of person who is uncomfortable wearing a tie unless it's absolutely necessary. We go back to knowing yourself well; what you can compromise on and what you really stand for. When you have a solid foundation of your personality, you can exude the credibility, integrity and charm inherent to you.

Let's put your ideas into words so that you have a visual reference of where you want your brand to go. List down your characteristics, preferably your strengths, and goals, and see if you can narrow them down in order to create a brand statement. Once that's settled, you can practice walking in those new pairs of shoes. You can creatively market yourself, you will need to adjust in the beginning, but you will soon get accustomed to your new lifestyle. You're living your dream life. In two weeks' time, you can feel the difference in your self-esteem. You are proactively living the life you want as an ambassador for your personal brand; it is natural to feel a surge of confidence. Embrace it!

We have discussed establishing positive first impressions. Now, how do we make it sustainable so that people can predict your next movc? When you become predictable, people feel al ease because they think they know you and that's a special connection right there. How can we maintain their perception of you?

You can refer to these questions for guidance:

1. What are you passionate about?
2. What is a skill or talent that comes naturally to you?
3. What part of your personality are you most proud of?
4. What are your core values in life?
5. What are your goals and what motivates you to achieve them?

Answering these questions will lead you to define the vision for your brand. This is a challenging process that will open your eyes to your true self. Some areas of your life might not be agreeable to you while there are areas that you will absolutely love. Enjoy this process of self-discovery and you will be closer to defining your personal brand.

What's next for you? You need a brand statement. It is the core of your brand which helps you identify what you stand for and allows you to be consistent with everything that you do.

Take this as an example: As a proficient global brand marketing executive with over a decade of experience, I have implemented cutting-edge marketing technologies that helped global retail and entertainment companies achieve aggressive growth in revenue through strategic marketing initiatives and successful campaigns.

You can list down your achievements or better yet, share your brand story. It gives people a clear image of who you are, your track record and your qualifications.

Is maintaining your personal brand difficult? The short answer is NO. The real answer is that it's challenging but definitely doable. Here are some ways that can help you do just that.

- Cultivate your skills and become adept in your field so people will look at you as an expert, and trust your recommendations.
- Help others by giving them sound advice about your field of expertise.
- Put yourself out there and maintain your constant presence by attending events and becoming a speaker so you can impart your knowledge.
- Establish your online presence through social media like Facebook, Instagram and LinkedIn etc.
- Be yourself at all times. Maintain a good reputation by helping people and avoiding words and actions that diminish your credibility.

A person who sticks to the core of who he is can be seen as authentic, influential, and credible. Live your life as genuinely as possible. Live your brand. And watch opportunities come your way from all directions.

4

REALIZE YOUR VISION

Declaring your vision of the future is simply a way of owning your dreams. It is similar to setting a goal for your brand so that you can be distinguished from all the other brands out there. In this next process of brand creation, we must be prepared to leave our comfort zone and write a brand vision that encapsulates the uniqueness of what you're offering your target audience. Your vision should be original. You can cultivate this perception by posting on your social media platforms about the development of your brand with consistency. You can observe and read the brand vision of other brands. Make sure that you do not copy their style. You are unique and different. You should be proud of that.

Where do you see your brand in 10 years? Is it thriving and conquering other markets? Are you expanding your reach? Your ambition for your brand should be apparent to your target audience so that people can support you while you anticipate the future. You don't wait for progress; you make things happen by defining your vision early on. It is the foundation of your brand. People will want to hire you or work with you if you are clear about the direction you want to take.

I hope you realize how important it is to state your brand vision from the beginning. By doing this, you are being open to more opportunities, more customers, a broader target market, and an online presence that spells longevity for your career. It's not a walk in the park, but your hard work will surely guarantee success for your brand.

FEATURE A UNIQUE SELLING POINT (USP)

Before you complete the whole picture of your personal brand, you have to outline your value proposition first. What is your unique selling point? What makes you a rare gem in a mine full of unformed diamonds? You can look at the brand of Apple. It's understated elegance. It's exquisite, but it doesn't hurt your eyes with too much flashiness. Apple has a distinct target market. The company is clear with their value proposition from the start.

Putting your rare qualities front and center can help you outshine other brands in your industry. Remember that having a unique vision is not just about yourself. It is a combination of your perception and your target audience's perception of your brand. Are you ready to begin creating your brand vision? Here are a few tips to help you out:

- Embrace your authenticity
- Know your guiding principles
- Be passionate about your talents
- Determine your rare qualities
- Listen to comments from people you trust
- List down your goals
- Launch your plan of action

The brand vision is a play of perceptions. How do you want your brand to be seen by people? Do you want them to look at your brand as a luxury brand? Or do you want to connect to the mass market? Your language when communicating with these two different groups should also vary.

What is it about you that is endearing to your target audience? Don't pretend that you love high-end or haute-couture when you are comfortable with a casual style. Don't use complicated words when you're adept at talking in an informal way. The key word is genuine. When you have accepted that you are who you are, it will be a breeze to formulate your brand vision.

Remember that you are human and you have qualities that other humans can relate to. The mistake is to think that you are superior to your target market. They will sense that in your marketing campaigns and even in how you speak to them through your social media platforms.

You have to be comfortable in your own skin. Some people are so ashamed of their flaws when clearly some of your shortcomings make you human and relatable. Don't hide them. If you have already discovered yourself, show yourself some dignity and show the world that you own your personality.

Allow me to walk you through this journey in redefining your vision for your personal brand. This list is going to help you move forward but don't confuse all of these items as rules or rigid laws. Some may or may not apply to your current circumstance, and it's up to your discretion to follow the ones that will be most beneficial to you.

TELL ME ABOUT YOURSELF

The above statement is predictable in job interviews or even social events. The person asking wants to know what you're all about in order to create more open communication and possibly, a strong connection.

If you want to create a personal brand, this essential statement has to have a ready answer. You must already be a master of yourself, so it's easy for you to tell people about yourself. If you are just starting out, it can make you uncomfortable, which is too be expected. Don't worry. It only takes practice. Self-awareness is an excellent tool for the realization of your vision.

HOW CAN I BE MORE SELF AWARE?

Define Your Values

Your values are the backbone of your entire self. They are your moral compass, dictating your life choices, directions, and decisions. What you perceive to be right and wrong is included in your core values. What aspects of your life carry more weight than others? When you list down your values, they include self-love, friendship, family, religion and other things that you hold dear.

Prioritizing Your Values

What do you think of your core values? How do you feel about them? It's important to ask yourself why you chose family over career. What motivates you to prioritize a certain value over the other? By delving deeper into your values and genuinely understanding your priorities, you can pretty much predict your decision-making process even in the future. This helps you become more self-aware which in turn guides you in building your brand.

Let's consider this situation. You have to make a decision between using children in the advertisement of your brand. Since you know that you value children and their future, you are very careful of portraying them positively in your ad. You cannot compromise that and let them be exploited even if it yields more money. Integrity over the money. You know your heart is in the right place and when people see your ad, they know that your brand cares for the welfare of children.

By staying true to your values, you are developing your personal brand in such a way that you are happy with how you handle your personal and professional life. You are a decent human being, and it shows in how you market your brand. In the end, your brand should bring you happiness. There are plenty of successful people who are not happy because they have compromised their values along the way, they have hurt and dishonored their family and friends. It's not a right way to live that's why having a clear list of your values, so you are on the right track at all times.

On the other hand, some people have dreams that took a back seat because they focused on building a better future for their families. When they reflected later on in their lives, they changed direction because they realized that they still have an opportunity to chase their dreams after helping their families. It's up to you. What do you value? What are you willing to sacrifice? As long as you are living your life with a positive disposition and not as a resentful person, then you can thrive and succeed.

Explore Your Passions

Passions are wide-ranging. They can be in music, arts, business, or politics. Now, what makes passion different from values? When it comes to passions, these are the things that you devote your time to and bring you immeasurable satisfaction. They fascinate you and thus make you more interested in doing them even for the rest of your life. Of course, your passions occupy your time, so you have to be careful which ones you want to explore. Since you have two passions, both personal and professional, it is only right that you incorporate them into your personal branding. Knowing your own passion can lead you to discover what your profession will be.

For example, if you are fond of drawing and creating, you can be a painter or an architect. If you are keen on numbers and equations, you can pursue a career in engineering. Travelling is a passion for many that is why you can see that there are many travel bloggers these days. They make a living out of their personal passions.

Discover Your Ideal Personality

Choosing your values and passions are essential in this journey that you now take to self-awareness. After you have accomplished them, you can move on to discovering your ideal personality.

Nowadays, you can find many personality tests that determine in which category of people you belong to. Are you an introvert or an extrovert? Are you emotional or rational? The Myer-Briggs personality test can give you an accurate estimate of your personality, but of course, each person is unique, so it is not a full-proof reference. Remember that in your broad personality there will be traits that are desirable and undesirable. When you identify them, you have the capacity to enhance your personality and look for areas of improvement.

Find Room for Improvement

Now, the next stage is uncomfortable for some people while there are others who will find it helpful. You have to open up to your family, friends and people whose judgment you value, and ask them to comment on your personality. What do they want you to improve on? What do they like about you? You might be surprised by their feedback at first, but if you look closely, you will eventually understand the areas that they are pointing to. It will be a sign of humility if you can accept their comments, reflect on them, and change what you can in order to be a better person.

What Can I See in My Future?

You have reached this final stage in creating your brand vision. Good job! Now we're off to stage two! This stage is exciting. It's about discovering where you want to be in the future. You probably have an idea of what you want to be. But is that really what you want? Is that something you'll be excellent at? Will that make you happy?

If you are ready and have a clear goal, well, then that's amazing! But if you don't, let's figure it out together. There are a few steps which will help you discover where you really want to be. For those who already have clear goals, it won't hurt if you also look into this guide, and re-evaluate them for your growth.

Rewards

The daily grind is not going to be grand because that's how it's supposed to be. You only celebrate the milestones, but when you are appreciative of your work and your current life, then you will be happier. Remember the moments when you felt happy and the projects that you find rewarding, and reflect on them.

Think about this. Are you happy when you achieve your professional goals? Do you like solving problems in the office? Is it fulfilling for you when you can express and share your ideas with others?

These questions also apply to your personal life. When you are not obligated to work, do you enjoy spending time with your family and sharing advice with your children? Isn't helping your daughter with homework a satisfying experience?

These professional and personal rewards are what makes your life complete. Make a list of these rewarding moments as motivation for you to go on and build a brand that resonates with who you are.

Creating a Brand Vision

Now, your list of the things that make you happy should be simplified and specified so that you can refer easily to it.

If your list is made up of positive qualities that you find in yourself, you can put labels on them to categorize them into a suitable profession. For example, you're good in public relations; you can be in human resources. You're family-oriented and enjoys teaching; you can be a pre-school teacher.

Imagine Your Career Pinnacle

Did you discover a career that will bring you happiness? By this time, you should have narrowed down a vague collection of all things that make you happy with something more specific. Perhaps, you have set your eyes on sales because you're good with people and you have a persuasive personality. What do you want to sell?

By becoming more self-aware in this exercise, you have already decided on selling real estate. Why is that? You like matching people with beautiful homes. You just enjoy the feeling of providing them with the right choice for a house that they will cherish for years.

Where do we go from here? To the future, of course! Now, write down what you can foresee of your career pinnacle. You have reached the apex of success. What are you doing in that scenario? Are you living in a modern two-storey house with a beautiful family? At this moment, are you going out of your car to meet your 250th client and you feel excited to find them an ideal property for their residence or commercial establishment? Visualization of the future is an excellent exercise to help you establish your brand vision. If the image is vivid, you feel more motivated to realize it.

Different Directions – One Destination

The future is all set; it's now time to return to the present moment. Let's ask the crucial question: How do you get from point A to point B? A being your current journey and B being your future success. This is an open secret: there are several paths leading to one destination. Remember that always so that when you fail in one path, you can dust yourself off and follow another path, both of which will lead you to your dream destination. But you will not move unless you choose one path. So choose wisely!

Revisiting Your Core Values

Since your brand vision is crystal clear now, you have to refer to your core values once again. Is your career plan consistent with your core values? Is pursuing your passion aligned with your guiding principles in life? I hope all the elements are interconnected so you can move forward with clarity of direction.

5

CRAFTING PERFECT BRAND PROMISE

We live in the modern world, and a brand promise has taken on a whole new meaning from its traditional concept. It transcends the benefits of a simple business tagline or slogan. Now, a brand promise is embraced as a way of life by consumers and the people, directly and indirectly, affected by it.

Coca-Cola has been a leading example of a brand promise that has evolved successfully over the years. Now, we associate it to a particular lifestyle; opening a bottle of coke is similar to bringing happiness in people's lives. It's remarkable! A brand promise that seeps into the heart and soul of the people it serves is a rarity. It is a goal that your personal brand can aim for. To say that it's a game-changer is an understatement. It is transcendental because its nature creates human ties which are difficult to break.

The brand impact has to be felt at different levels including emotional, social, and even environmental. It is undoubtedly a holistic approach to branding especially with the arrival of globalisation in society. You don't just affect one person; you affect entire communities and even nations. Their experience of a specific brand should endure through the years. For a person who's just starting out, this may seem overwhelming, but you have to aim higher even if you begin with little steps first.

Think of your brand promise as a raw material to build a corporation or even an empire. By defining your promise, you can deduce your mission and vision for your personal brand. These elements will soon come together to showcase your compelling brand story. The people who feel an emotional and social affinity to your goals will naturally embrace your purpose-driven promise.

In today's generation where great ideas inspire collective action, people are drawn to brands that engage and captivate them on so many levels. Through these concepts, appealing and transformative brands have a more significant impact thus garnering higher profitability than those brands who are not giving much effort to connect deeply with their target base.

You can observe this thirst for meaning not just from consumers but also the people who are involved in your brand. Your staff, employees, and business partners are motivated to collaborate and promote your brand because they believe deep down that it brings value to the community as a whole.

Your brand promise attracts like-minded individuals in your company or organization. It keeps you on your toes and ensures that your direction to growth and progress is on track. Within your organization and with outside competition, you are much more focused on a concrete brand promise.

HOW YOUR BRAND PROMISE AFFECT YOUR BUSINESS?

A clearly defined and purpose-driven brand promise has a powerful impact on your business. It becomes an umbrella where all the plans and concepts of your brand are covered, and all the stakeholders are underneath doing everything possible to fulfil your promise. Every action within your business is done in a cohesive, cooperative and systematic way because your brand promise ties everything together.

Your brand promise becomes a driving force that dictates the perceptions and attitudes of every staff or employee in your business. It harmonizes your work culture within the company and directs your marketing and advertising campaigns. Certainly, your productivity reaches a higher level because of the commitment of everyone in your team to come up with great and innovative ideas and products.

In the core of your brand is a promise that tugs at the heart of consumers and they no longer just consume, they enjoy and relish the experience hence they want to be a part of it. Every element of your business is impacted positively, and you as the founder are transformed as well. The way you live is consistent with your brand promise which radiates a truth that many people aspire to emulate and embrace.

Highlighting your brand promise becomes the realization of the dreams of the consumers. Through your brand, they can see that it is possible to achieve their goals in life as well, to live their purpose, to live fully because someone has already proven it to them. The people on your team think, feel, and believe that what they do has an enormous impact on the society they belong to. Your brand promise strengthens your bond with the people you directly influence and the ones that are affected by your presence.

People remember your brand more than any other because it has touched their lives and they want to share that experience with their loved ones. This movement creates ripple effects and the next thing you know; you have touched a million lives.

WHAT CAN YOU PROMISE?

Nowadays, it is not enough to have a brand promise that will not be sustainable and relevant to society. Starting a personal brand cannot be done on a whim. There's a lot of planning that goes into it. Ask the more established brands like Coca-Cola, Nike, Apple, etc. They have reputations to uphold. They need to keep their brand promise 100% of the time. In starting out, you have to set high standards as well.

Your brand was created with a purpose, and it has to show in every way from advertising, promoting, selling to following up. Your brand promise must be visible at all times so that your brand will remain in people's hearts and minds.

HOW CAN YOU FULFILL YOUR BRAND PROMISE?

Your brand has its own personality, and a brand promise should reflect that. Your promise should be fulfilled with every single encounter you have with a customer or with a member of your team. Stick to your brand promise, and eventually, it will become part of your personal and professional life.

You have to deliver consistently or else you will lose your credibility. People expect you to deliver and you have to meet their expectations. It is tedious and exhausting at times that's why from the very start, you have to craft a brand promise that can maintain its longevity.

HOW TO MAKE BRAND PROMISE UNFORGETTABLE?

Consistency, as mentioned earlier, is vital in fulfilling a brand promise. But how can you make people remember your brand for a long time? The answer is visibility. Your brand has to be on people's radar regularly. Social media can help you here. It is a great tool to utilize in order to stay in touch with your target audience. Learn to promote your brand through different channels online as well as offline. Today, the best way to do it is to create your own website and have your social media platforms link up to this website. This allows your posts to be seen by a wider audience. Remember that the internet is a powerful place to expand your reach. It is global. Take advantage of it!

Since we talked about your website, you have to take into account the visuals and designs. They must be consistent with your brand. Stick to one logo and one colour scheme. As a beginner, you might want to try several options first before settling on the final choice. When that is done, you can market your brand by sending e-mails, newsletter, press releases, e-books, etc. With the final designs incorporated people will be able to identify your brand with regular exposure just like the famous car brands you see around: Ford, Chevrolet, Hyundai, etc.

MAKE YOUR BRAND MEMORABLE AND UNIQUE

Show the world that your brand has something different to offer. Success may make your brand grow, but your brand promise remains unalterable. You keep your integrity, and the people will trust you even more. They will associate reliability and integrity with your brand.

There are two fundamental concepts that you need to consider in making your brand promise unique: the visual perception and the intangible vision. You are already familiar with the visual aspects which include the logo and design, or what people see directly. Now, let's familiarize ourselves with what the eyes can't see, but the heart can comprehend:

- **Bringing value to people's lives**

From the beginning, you have to know what value you can offer the people you wish to serve. You could bring them happiness, security, hope, warmth or any other essential human emotion through your brand. You are not just presenting a product or service; you are also providing something of benefit to the people.

Now creating products or delivering services that are already valuable can affect the lives of your customers positively is not the end of the journey. You have to communicate this value so that people, your target audience, will understand what you're offering. You can't just hard sell them on anything. It's essential to build rapport and communicate through telling a story. Working with a vast global company can feel impersonal, but your interactions with clients can be personal. It is up to you to make it so. You have control over your own impact on the people you serve directly.

- **Strategizing for better branding**

Tons of hard work is put into making a personal brand shine, no matter what's the size of your business. If you just dedicate yourself to the unique value that you possess and focus on that your brand will become more engaging and persuasive. When the foundation is built you can launch your brand in a way that people will find memorable. By getting one foot inside the door, you are also getting your brand in people's hearts. The rest will be a matter of reaching out time and again to remain visible and relevant. Let's talk about how we can take all these steps one by one:

I. Observe and Discover

Be a keen observer. Pay attention to trends and feel the people's pulse on certain issues, products, cultures, and phenomenon. This will give you a glimpse of the needs and wants of your target audience. Then you can ask yourself, where do I come in? What kind of value can I provide that these people will be able to benefit from? Am I good at giving customized solutions to people's complex problems? Answering these questions will lead to the discovery of your purpose and how you can transform that into a great career. Talk to people, reach out by conducting surveys, ask mentors, and communicate with people you trust for feedback.

II. Focus and Highlight

For example, a dietician determined that her unique value to her patient was personal attention. How did she know? Simple, she asked her patients. Few patients said that they valued the extra time and effort she spends explaining the details of weight management and helping them even with recipes.

There was an actor who felt as if he had something more to offer. He talked to his directors, his mentors, and his fan base to learn about talents that he can share. He found out he's a good motivator and role model for others who have also struggled. Armed with his experience speaking with people and motivating them, he became a life coach. Gradually, his purpose became clear to him, and the people around him were also grateful that he is helping them with their dreams.

III. Share and Communicate

It's an act of generosity to share what you know and communicate with your target audience. By doing so, you are creating a connection that may be personal at first but can turn into a professional relationship in the future. You have to invest in communication because this is a powerful and persuasive tool that can influence people to become part of your professional circle.

IV. Grow and Develop

You create your own business to fulfill your purpose in life and to achieve productivity and profitability to sustain your lifestyle as well. Building a personal brand makes the realization of these dreams possible.

There are stages in the development process that you should take into account. You cannot go into this blindfolded. You should be ready to invest money, time, effort, and even your entire life for a period of time to launch your personal brand and manage it. Remember not to stagnate and always keep the growth consistent.

6

MAKING DISTINCTIVE PERSONAL BRAND

Are you the first, the best, or the different one in the marketplace? What makes you distinct from the competition? Successful branding means distinction, originality, and standing out from the rest. Whether it's a product or service, what is it that you do that sets your apart? Is your service or product a level higher than what can be found in the market? Or is it one of a kind? Either way, you will attract buyers.

Pay attention to the relevance of your brand to the people you want to reach out to. Does it have a rare appeal? The purpose of your brand is to provide value to others which include consumers and clients. Your branding may start with you; it may talk about you, but the target is the other side of the spectrum which is the people who will buy, avail of your services or work with you. They want to know how your services or products are going to be useful to them.

So, bring out your unique talents, competencies, and traits, and package them while keeping the consumer/audience in mind in order to form a reliable brand. It's worth remembering that Warren Buffet imparted this knowledge, "Your premium brand had better be delivering something special, or it's not going to get the business".

Embracing the ethical standards of personal branding is tantamount to your success. If you want to achieve long-term prosperity, it's crucial that you respect the rights of others and conduct business in a respectable and trustworthy way. Only then can you be satisfied with the taste of triumph. Your personal brand should be a reflection of the kind of person who worked tirelessly in order to create it.

The success of the great and popular brands out there is based on other intangible things such as integrity, dedication, authenticity, and a customer-centric approach. By helping people and going the extra mile, you will reap the rewards of your hard work. High profits come after you have proven that you can help people enhance and uplift their lives.

In business and in almost every profession, there is a term called best practices. This is a crucial element to developing your personal brand. When you are committed to the best practices every time you are interacting with a client or serving a customer, you ensure the best experience they can have while connecting with your brand. You have to keep your brand promise at all times and keep it close to your heart as well. Don't forget your integrity when you are tested.

It is essential that you stand firm because you are carrying your brand with every encounter with stakeholders, customers, family and friends, peers, and even strangers who you can transform into clients. Now you have to keep some reminders in your office and take the time to review them when the need arises. I'm sharing some valuable tips that would be impactful in your personal branding initiative:

COMBINE RATIONAL AND EMOTIONAL ASPECTS

For your personal brand to become more recognizable and relatable, you should have a right mix of the elements of the heart and mind that other human beings, your target audience, will be able to share a connection with. You use your brain for rationality and your heart for emotional empathy. When you give people logical reasons to patronize your brand, you are appealing to their rational side. To complete the picture, you also have to reach out to them emotionally to pull at their heartstrings.

Striking a balance between the rational and emotional side is helpful in having a holistic impact on people. A personal brand that caters to both sides becomes endearing to people. It becomes an entity that people resonate with just as they do a friend or a family. They feel comfortable with your brand, connected and understood.

TAKE ADVANTAGE OF THE POWER OF SOCIAL MEDIA

Communication media these days are modern, streamlined, and fast. Each communication online can be done in real time. You can chat and talk to anyone from another country. If you take advantage of this opportunity to differentiate your brand from the rest then the best platform would be social media. You can post regularly about the updates happening in your brand or business. Some of the businesses offline have no online presence, but you will not follow that path. You have to establish a strong online presence so that you are visible to your target audience. Maintain open communication with them. You have to begin somewhere, and when you create a LinkedIn profile, you can expect that your contact list will be longer and there are so many possibilities for employment, work collaboration, opportunities etc.

DON'T DULL YOUR SPARKLE

Some businesses don't succeed because they are afraid of the spotlight. You cannot have the same fate as failed businesses because they refuse to adapt to the changing times. You have to build a door of opportunities if it is not knocking on yours at the moment. Be clear with your vision and avoid mediocre people who don't wish to succeed. Use your time wisely in building your own personal brand. Take pride in what you can do and what you have already accomplished. You will attract achievers and successful people as well.

EMBRACE ORIGINALITY

The reason you built a personal brand is to be noticed and stand out. Even with so many people around you being a copycat, don't follow in their footsteps. You may want to look like or be like a specific famous brand, but you cannot be able to keep up in the long run because it is not original, your unique image and identity is more important. It is not worth it to lose your credibility as a reputable brand if you only wish to copy what others have been doing.

Believe that your brand has a chance to shine and succeed. You can be original and successful. The path that a lot of brands have taken may be more convenient to take, but you have to forge ahead on your own. Look to yourself and embrace the unique qualities that you have. With billions of people on this earth, it is logical to consider that there are millions of people who are like-minded and like-hearted. You will find your target audience, and you will have stronger ties that can create meaningful collaboration in the future.

BRANDING IS CHOOSING WISELY

Life is a competition in all aspects. You compete within the family, in school and the workplace. There is someone fit for a particular role. You are given a unique gift, and you have a special role to play. Your goal is to find that role. When you are unfit for the role that you play in your personal or professional life, you will be unhappy, so you have to make choices every single day. Choose to be happy. Select the paths that will lead you to a more consistent personal brand, the ones that reflect your true self and your own dreams, only then can you be authentic with your brand.

Now, I will help you with more tips to growing your brand rapidly. Let's take a look at the things you can do on social media:

Empowering Your Brand Through Social Media

By using social media platforms, you can share your blog posts, stories, expert tips, offers and share the best content. If you're not ready using these social media platforms, I would recommend trying Facebook, Twitter, Instagram and LinkedIn first.

- Share meaningful professional or personal photos on Instagram. It's the easiest platform to share compelling stories about your brand so that you can further introduce yourself to your target audience. Build relationships with people who have shared interests through this platform. Embrace your artistic side and use popular image apps to make a distinct look for your images. Use relevant hashtags so that people will be able to find you easily especially people in your field of endeavor.

- Use your LinkedIn profile wisely. Employers do their prospecting on the online these days. With a complete and comprehensive profile, you have a higher chance of being noticed by potential clients and employers especially the ones who can match your skills and experience to an ideal job. Opportunities about in LinkedIn and you have to take advantage of the wide-ranging list of contacts that you can reach out to. Through LinkedIn, you can talk to CEOs and HR personnel of big companies. You can also build your contact list by scanning through the profiles of people in your industry.

Use LinkedIn Efficiently

- Add relevant people to your contact lists such as peers, colleagues, and former teachers and classmates etc.
- Add a minimum of 5 references from people who you are confident have positive observations and recommendations for you.
- Complete your profile. I can't stress this enough. If the people visiting your profile can see from first glance precisely what your personal brand is all about, you are already persuading to hire you or work with you on future projects.

Create A Powerful Facebook Profile

Do you already have a Facebook profile? Is it a personal account? I recommend that you create another one for your professional profile even if you will use it for your personal branding. Through that account, you can create a Facebook page wherein you showcase your professional achievements and track record. This is the first step to establishing your credibility online. Now, let's take a look at some of the way you can use to build your personal brand through Facebook:

- ❖ Find a topic that you are passionate about, and you have sufficient knowledge of.
- ❖ Introduce a link to your website every time you have written a blog so that people can follow the link and learn about your latest offerings.
- ❖ Take pride in sharing videos, pictures, and ideas through Facebook regarding your stand on certain issues so that your followers can relate to your message.
- ❖ Expound on this topic and share relevant posts or blogs as an informational tool to the people who follow you.

Master YouTube Marketing

YouTube is a flexible platform that is popular with marketers. You can create your own channel and let your followers subscribe so that you can keep them posted on all things related to your brand. Here are a few tips for a successful YouTube branding:

- ❖ Create videos that give advice or share recommendations.
- ❖ You can make an infomercial and upload on YouTube or create a video with yourself as the narrator and presenter.
- ❖ Upload high-quality videos so that your visuals can help your message be more easily understood. Don't limit yourself to professional content. You can feature fun videos as well.
- ❖ Believe that you can create content which people will love and subscribe, too. Be brave in putting yourself

out there especially if you're an artist and you want to break into the showbiz world.

- YouTube is perfect for coaches because they can upload their webinars or online courses on the channel for free. They can just put a link to their website so that the marketing funnel will still continue. All they have to do is persuade their followers to visit their websites through the videos.

Marketing Is Alive On Twitter

This modern world is all about sound bites. With 280 characters or less, you can already sell your personal brand. Of course, you don't want to be annoying to your followers hence you have to engage them like a reasonable person who has a Twitter account. Diversify the contents that you post otherwise, your target audience will be bored with what you post. Below are some helpful recommendations for your Twitter marketing:

- First, you have to follow the trailblazers in your industry so that you will remain up-to-date with what's currently happening.
- Like and retweet posts that are consistent to your personal brand. If you are into baking desserts, make sure that your Twitter posts are related to the topic. But don't post too often and let your followers miss you a little bit.
- Strategize properly and use hashtags so that the people who need to know about your brand can easily find you.
- Establish connections on Twitter by commenting positively in the posts of others.
- Observe proper etiquette when dealing with people on Twitter and other social media accounts. Respect

begets respect. Show that your brand is respectable.

Discover the Advantage of Google+

Increasingly, people are growing accustomed to using Google+. They like the fact that it is easy to share content through this medium. You can study how Google+ works and learn about its many helpful features. You can check Google Keyword Search which is beneficial to understanding the keywords to use for your personal branding. Your website or social media accounts will be more accessible if you use valid keywords. It takes time to learn about Google+, but the advantages are well worth your time and effort.

Now, I think you will find these tips useful in managing your social media profiles.

1. Have you considered organizing all your social media account in one place? To be honest, it is quite tedious to manage all of them individually. It takes up so much of your time, and you also have other activities to think about. I suggest you try using Hootsuite as a central dashboard where you can streamline all your updates for your social media profiles including Facebook and Twitter. Everything is integrated, and you can control your updates by using your smartphone. You are free to check your posts and monitor your progress anywhere in the world especially if you are the type of person who is always travelling and on the go.

2. Of course, the contents of your social media accounts have to be organized, and I don't think you want to be redundant or repetitive with your tasks. About.me can help you access all your social profiles in one place only. This will help you with your bios and business descriptions if necessary.

3. Some people don't want to voice out their opinions for fear of being shut down. With a personal brand, you have to be more proactive. Find interesting online platforms where you can have meaningful exchange and banters with other people. You don't know who you might meet in a Facebook group. You can use such tools such as Twitter Search and Google Alerts to identify more about what's going on so that you can participate as well. Sometimes, by commenting on a fascinating article you might meet a like-minded individual involved in a company or organization that you want to be a part of. It all revolves around networking with the right people.

7

IMPROVE YOUR VALUE PROPOSITION

Your brand is no longer just about marketing and selling. In recent years, we have redefined the meaning of the personal brand. It has become more meaningful with entrepreneurs, businesses, and companies reaching out to people not to get something from them but to provide value. They are more open to an exchange of good ideas between sellers and customers. You may have observed that proliferation of advertisements that focus on the customer's needs and wants these days. How can you make a difference in people's lives? That is a difficult question to ask that requires careful thought before answering.

Now to show appreciation for our clients and customers, you should choose a more impactful route in dealing with them, in connecting with them. Listen closely to their feedback and if you hear compliments, list them down, too. Don't be too critical of your brand and avoid always finding fault. Embrace the good qualities that your target audience points out. When you do this, you balance your own perception of your brand. There are constructive comments that will really help you improve and there are also positive feedbacks that can boost your confidence and inspire gratitude in you.

What can you take away from positive feedbacks?

The benefits of getting positive feedbacks are plenty. You become more motivated to work harder and serve better when you hear a compliment. Have you noticed how your staff becomes more cheerful when you pay him or her a compliment? It is the same with your brand. The positive energy is invigorating.

To take full advantage of positive feedbacks, you can also list them all down after you hear them from customers and clients. You should also take note of the positive comments from peers and business partners. As soon as you have listed down these positive statements, you can identify the recurring themes and find out how to consolidate them so that you can utilize them for your branding and marketing. Sometimes, you can make a business tagline upon hearing a sincere compliment from a customer.

Now, you may have a strong opinion of your brand and what direction you want to take with it, but you should accept the comments of others, too. You have a blind spot and your customers and clients can see some areas that you may have overlooked. Respect their opinions and if they are open to the opportunity, you can delve deeper and ask them how you can make everything better.

ENCHANCE YOUR VALUE PROPOSITION

Based on the feedback that you received, you can review your value proposition and adjust accordingly. Listen to your mentors and ask them regarding your biggest strengths which would stem from their perception of you. Be prepared for some negative feedbacks as well. Life is not all fun and positivity. You have to be strong to face the downsides and learn from them.

If you want to develop your value proposition further, you can look to your fan base, audience, or contact list. Send e-mails to your contacts, peers, and customers and make a simple survey by asking them short questions regarding your services, products, or your brand. When you receive their replies, be more objective in reading the comments. You can categorize them into positive, negative, and can be improved. You can have someone you trust to do this task for you in order to lend it more objectivity. Don't edit anything in this early stage of the development. Just put all the similar comments together so that you can review and analyze them later on.

Let's have a look at some of the similar comments in a category:

Open communication

- Attentive to the needs of the customers
- Listened to complaints without interruption
- Explained the situation clearly
- Offered excellent solutions and recommendations
- Respected the decision of the clients

It's good to have these positive comments sorted out and validated because it intensifies your value proposition. Noting down these great feedbacks reinforce the credibility and importance of your brand. After compiling them all, you can rank these feedbacks by order of importance and you can deduce what qualities of your brand people love. It's an eye-opening exercise that can truly improve your branding initiative.

You can show your consolidated list to people you trust especially mentors who are active in the industry. Go to your friends who are industry experts and verify the validity of your findings. This makes the process come full circle. In the end, you can take some time off and review this by yourself. After collaborating with people, it's important that you sit down and consider your own opinion on the matter. You have your own perception and the perception of other people to assess and analyze. This put you in a better position to formulate a game plan for your brand development. Certainly, these inputs will be the foundation of your value proposition.

Your value proposition should be the heart of your career strategy. Below are three crucial steps you can follow to develop a strong value proposition:

1. **Clear Purpose:** The value proposition begins with a purpose, one that needs what you have to offer. Once you understand your goal, it will be easy for you to focus correctly on your target market.

2. **Know Your Strengths:** It is obvious, when building a personal brand you must know your strengths so how can we ignore it while developing value proposition. Your strengths should act as the foundation of your value proposition. Showcase your strengths, don't wait for clients and employers to figure out.

3. **Success Stories:** Your clients and employers will be paying you because of your value propositions mean your strengths and purpose. Create an impact by showcasing your success stories, so it makes your case convincing. Put together facts on a measurable scale such as growth or cost reduction etc.

THE SIGNIFICANCE OF YOUR VALUE PROPOSITION

A well-crafted value proposition propels your personal brand forward and further down the road to success. Since you have your values in check, your actions and decisions will be influenced greatly by them. All the progress and plans for your brand and your team will emanate from your value proposition. You will achieve your goals with clarity, precision, and success!

8

POSITIONING YOUR BRAND PROPERLY

Brands evolve as consumer's behaviours change and adapt to the progress of society. A good strategy for brand positioning should embrace this fundamental concept. Relating to the needs of the people at a particular time is necessary and sustaining that adaptability through the years is essential for all brands and businesses. By remaining static and not being able to adapt, a brand risks becoming irrelevant in the eyes of its target market.

The influence of brands over consumer receptivity and behaviour is great, and marketers and advertisers are well aware of such power. Modern marketing techniques have become more complex, and everything has to be customized to a particular audience otherwise you will be isolating people from a specific demographic. Marketing is becoming an art of connection between sellers and consumers, not just ordinary connections but relevant and empathetic connections.

Successful brands are correctly managed, with all aspects meticulously assessed and analyzed so that when they are presented to the public, they tell a cohesive story and compelling story. There is definitely overcrowding in our capitalist and consumerist world hence brand positioning is even more vital in this day and age.

We have reverted to being humanists, and a more personal approach is much more appreciated compared to the traditional formal interaction. Brands have to establish their originality, their engagement, and their capacity to persuade their target market. As a brand creator, you have to launch a trademark for your personality and key qualities. Be extraordinary and watch all eyes fixed on you!

After all, that's said and done. You have to take into consideration your unique value as you position your brand correctly. You can't please everybody no matter what you do. It is best to focus on a specific niche and devote all your energies to making your following grow in that area but without ignoring brand awareness. Don't forget brand awareness comes before target markets. Who is part of your target market? If they read about you or read your posts on social media, will they be captivated or will they feel as if you are not speaking to them directly? Tread lightly and know your target audience genuinely in order to navigate these unpredictable waters.

Let's position your brand better with these useful tips:

Create a specific Facebook page: People online LIKE social media pages that post updates about things that are relevant to them. They get their daily dose of information from Facebook, and if they see your brand regularly updating your page, they will most likely engage with you. You provide useful information, and you grow your following. Win-Win Situation!

Present a clear message: In your social media profiles, describe your offering as clearly as possible. Make sure that it's the first thing people see when they visit your website or

LinkedIn profile. Keep it short and simple.

Describe your position immediately: Don't beat around the bush. Tell people exactly what you do and your strengths. After that, you can engage them by giving out advice and recommendations in your area of expertise.

Communicate your story well: Go out there and promote your brand by telling stories about it. If you can join seminars, events, fundraising campaigns, and other social events in order to meet people and build your network, do it soon. Establish connections with people who share the same ideas and goals. Show them that you are open to new ventures and you can help them if they need advice or solutions. Be accessible to your target audience. They will notice and remember your presence.

ALL ABOUT POSITIONING

You have a unique voice and style and how you position that to be noticed by everybody is up to you. It can be done in a lot of ways. You can market your brand in traditional or contemporary ways as long as you stay true to your brand identity. Since there are plenty of new marketing strategies and techniques, it would be wise to select your strategy and stick to the best.

THE AGE OF NEW IDEAS

Ideas run within a cycle. They are created, enhanced, reborn, and so forth. What you need to do to capture the most productive part of the cycle is to pay attention to what's happening in the world currently. There are new ideas, techniques, opportunities, learning methods, and careers.

These innovations are products of the imaginative minds of human beings, and your brand will benefit from a makeover or even just a simple transformation.

Businesses, both online and offline, undergo website changes, physical renovations, and location expansion. We are on the verge of seeing a world of new opportunities and in the world of branding, it is the same. We have to step up our game and position our brands by utilizing new techniques and marketing methods.

QUICK RECAP

Why develop your personal brand?

- To uncover your professional purpose
- To get heard and noticed
- To become more noticeable to stakeholders
- To boost brand engagement
- To increase customers
- To boost the sales
- To establish a strong online presence
- To open the doors of opportunities
- To increase your fan base, followers and supporters
- To get your dream career and live the life you want
- To provide value to the community you belong to
- To establish yourself as an expert in your industry
- To grow your network
- And become global

ESSENTIAL TIPS TO GET YOU STARTED

1. Define your objectives clearly so that your team knows the exact direction.
2. Discover if you are well-equipped with knowledge and experience.
3. Compensate for the lack of knowledge by training, studying, and working.
4. Observe your target audience and figure out how you can make an impact.
5. Present your value offering and evaluate people's response.
6. Recalibrate your strategy as needed in order to retain more customers.

EFFECTS OF CULTURE IN PERSONAL BRANDING

Cultural differences affect the way a brand is perceived. In a certain culture, a brand may be famous, but in another, its message may not be well-received. Knowledge of the culture of your target audience is an advantage. You have to learn how to adjust to the traditions and perceptions of the people you want to serve such as your employers, customers, clients, and stakeholders.

We have to be aware of the taboos of certain cultures. If we can adapt to these rules, our customers can only respect us in return. Your personal brand should be more empathetic and must respect diversity.

HOW CAN WE DEAL WITH CULTURAL DIFFERENCES?

Your brand has to show that you accept the differences in culture. It's important for people to know that you don't discriminate anyone no matter what religion, tradition or race. Show genuine interest to understand the nuances of culture and adjust your marketing content to suit the preference of your target audience. Through your brand, you can create a culture that is uniquely your own. Being a social influencer means that people believe your message and follow your footsteps.

KEY ADVICE TO BOOST YOUR PERSONAL BRAND

1. Craft a Captivating Design

Designing your logos, headers and all the visuals of your website in a cohesive way is very important. The design represents the personality and style of your brand. You have to decide on a final style and design before you insert the contents.

2. Be in the First Page of Google

Being visible in search engines especially Google is a huge plus for your marketing and advertising initiative. Pay attention to search engine optimization and how to boost your presence online. When people search your industry online, your website will be on the first page of Google and people will be able to visit your website immediately.

3. Hire a Professional to Work on Your Brand

You have to invest in your personal brand and most of the time this means you have to shell out money to hire professionals. Hire a talented web designer if necessary. Consult your mentors so that they can recommend a trustworthy professional.

4. Promote through Social Media

Positioning through social media is can be a very efficient and successful method if you know how to use the platforms properly. Sometimes, it works to be formal and professional in your approach to clients especially if your field is law or politics. However, if you are into business and your target market is composed of younger people, you have to adapt to their language as well. Utilize Google, Facebook and LinkedIn so that you can capitalize on these influential social media platforms.

9

LAUNCHING YOUR BRAND POSITIVELY

In career development programs, experts are introducing the concept of the personal instead of the professional identity. Being cooperative with a group and being part of company culture is still relevant but there is more emphasis on individuality now. Clients and Employers hire people who have a personal brand because their leadership and initiative is apparent. By building their online presence, they are easily accessible which exhibits signs of willingness to work and accomplish projects on their own. These are desirable traits that the workforce is looking for.

Popular brands that have endured years of constant change in the industry leave lasting memories for customers. They have stories to tell, memories to impart, social cultures to share. They have established an extraordinary impact on their target audience, and sometimes the effect is personal. An individual has been affected in one way or another with a specific brand of car, clothes, jewellery, etc. Brands are just the products of the imaginations of their creators and guess what, their creators are people. Here lies the secret of powerful marketing. It all comes down to people.

When you finally launch your brand, remember that you are communicating with people. They are the one you should please. No checklist in the world could encompass everything a human being needs hence you should open your eyes and be more observant. People want to feel and experience a brand as deeply as possible. You may have watched commercials that inspire happy and blissful emotions. They center around the value of a brand to the lives of the consumers.

Strategic Brand Management author, Prof. Kevin Lane Keller, relates that marketers promote the element of being unforgettable in order to induce recall or recognition of a certain brand. You have made a great impression, and people want to get to know your brand further. They want to find out if they can trust you? It's crucial that they rely on your integrity. Customers want to believe that you care about their welfare and whatever you are offering will change their lives for the better.

Forget about marketing strategies that insult the emotional intelligence of buyers and customers. For marketers, you have to understand that the people you want to sell to also possess a mind that can discern fakery and authenticity. You have to be careful and make a commitment to not deceive your customers.

BRAND RETENTION

There are thousands of brands out there, and perhaps you can only recall a hundred of them. But when you see their logos, you instantly recognize them. If your brand has high retention rate, this means that people can recall it. How can they remember it? Your marketing efforts may have worked. You may have done something to make your brand stick. What did you do? What methods did you incorporate in marketing?

Most of the time, it is the visual effect that captivates them especially for people who watch a lot of television. Their brains can select which brands are better based on their own biases as well. If you see a brand logo all the time, chances are you will recall it when you look at it again even in a foreign country. You feel like you're close to home upon seeing a brand logo that is familiar to you even as a child.

Of course, multinational companies go the extra mile in order to promote their brand. They have the money to invest in ads that are shown on television several times a day. Having the capacity to pay celebrities to endorse their products and services is also a plus factor. Small and medium-sized companies tend to go the traditional route. They advertise in local magazines and newspapers. But the internet is a game changer. Suddenly, every brand has the chance to shine globally even with just a social media platform.

Social media is inexpensive. If there ever were a tool that is so effective yet budget-friendly, it would have to be social media. You don't have to invest a lot of money to have a marketing program running these days. Of course, the big companies still have an edge because they can hire experts to create their social media ads for them. They can employ managers to monitor their Facebook, Twitter and Instagram accounts. On top of that, they have the means to pay for celebrities to post updates on their brands and business for them.

Everybody is on social media now. Even governments and presidents of the most powerful nations have access to social media. They know people all over the globe are tuned in and waiting for their updates. It is indeed a great way to communicate.

When it comes to your personal branding, you have to embrace the change. Don't ever feel intimidated by all the efforts of the huge companies. You can start small with your online presence. In fact, you should feel like you've hit the jackpot because you can communicate with anybody online these days even your dream mentors. It's incredible how the world has evolved, and it continues to grow for more connectivity and global unity, at least that is our most profound hope.

CLOSER CONNECTIVITY

Fortunately, the internet has levelled the playing field. Your brand can create your own story and share it with the world with just a few clicks of the mouse. There's also an Edit button which can help you formulate your stories and ideas better. The world gives you plenty of chances to make mistakes and rise from the ashes.

Since the global community is more interconnected these days, societal issues in every part of the world are known everywhere. Hence, you can also observe that the consumer behaviour of the present generation is very much affected. Now, everyone wants to climb mountains and commune with nature. This is another market for businesses. There is a need for better outdoor gears and clothing.

If you are keen on all these new trends, you can figure out a way to market your brand and sell your products with a clear intent of providing value. Each product or brand has to be eco-friendly and must be manufactured through ethical methods. The people show more compassion to others, the culture is different now. And as soon as you realize this shift, you can cater to your customers with more empathy too. You can connect to them on an emotional level.

Through social media, you can take a stand and your brand will be perceived in a different light. We no longer need brands that only care about profit. Today, consumers are looking at brands and assessing if their social and civic initiatives align with their own. Greed is not attractive. Compassion, humility, and a sense of shared belief in hope are widely accepted. Launch your brand in a way that unites your target audience. Show them that you care not just about personal success but also about the holistic growth of society.

10

MAINTAIN AND GROW YOUR BRAND

How do you maintain your personal brand?

A personal brand has three essential purposes. First of all, it is the perfect medium to use to attract valuable employers or attract clients, a dream job that fits your skill set and career goals. Secondly, a brand of your own gives you complete control of your online presence and strengthens your desired reputation. Lastly, it establishes you as an authority in your industry, a role that can bring new opportunities your way.

It all depends on how much effort you are willing on a daily basis for the development of your personal brand. For example, you can develop a blog to share your expertise and use social media to get your name out there. Or, you can just build your professional relationships through your social media.

FIVE EFFECTIVE WAYS TO MAINTAIN YOUR BRAND

1. Commit to your brand

You've put in all your effort to establish your personal brand, why would you let it go waste? When you encounter obstacles blocking your branding efforts, you shouldn't let your personal brand take the hit. You will lose a lot by being inconsistent and having an on-and-off attitude toward your work.

Recommendations:

Carve some uninterrupted time every single day to grow your brand, and stick to the schedule as much as you can. Don't worry if you miss a day or activity from time to time. You can compensate on other days and balance your efforts to remain on track.

Your turn! Reflect on the question below:

How do you stay true to your personal brand?

Do you ever feel like giving up on it?

How do you maintain your commitment?

2. Know your limits

I recommend discerning your limitations from the very beginning. They provide standards that you have to live up to. As your brand grows, remind yourself of your limits so that they will dictate your actions. It is expected that these limits can evolve over time. While it's important to be ready to interact, and build your personal brand, you won't be as effective if you push yourself too far.

Recommendations:

If you have any conflicts interfering with your personal brand, learn how to compensate. Know when to say No to your branding efforts to keep yourself burning out. On the other hand, decide when to prioritize your brand over other activities.

Your turn! What are your thoughts on the questions below?

Can you identify activities that interfere with your personal branding?

What hindrance do you face which affects your quality of work?

How do you balance your branding with work, family and other commitments?

3. Learn to step away

Everyone is working on their brand, including myself, you can get sucked because of overindulgence from time to time. We all have branding responsibilities that we try to meet every day, but being overwhelmed can cause multiple issues, image these scenarios:

You will experience burnout, causing you to make huge mistakes.

You can miss opportunities to enjoy the offline world.

You'll harm your body and affect your health by staying on the computer all day.

An essential part of maintaining your brand is learning to walk away when necessary so that you can refresh your mind and body.

Recommendations:

Go outside for a walk for a breath of fresh air. Another great idea is to hit the gym or read the recreational book. Do something different and healthy especially an activity that involves social interaction such as spending time with family and friends. Don't let your life pass by without experiencing it to the fullest.

Your turn! Recall your experlences

Have you ever completely burned out while working on your personal brand?

What are you planning to do to prevent that from happening (again)?

Do you have any strategies in place that you would recommend to others?

4. Schedule your posts

You have content ready for social media sharing, right? I bet you want to ensure you reach as many people as possible when you publish your post on social media. Unfortunately, it's not possible for you to be online 24/7 and publish everything manually, or respond to all replies and comments. While it's in your best interest to not fully automate your posts and tweet, you also need to be human and have a personal life.

Recommendations:

Use a scheduling tool to share tweets and posts according to custom settings. Take advantage of automation tools for your blog activity and email marketing. You need to find the right balance between automation and real-time activity. The best approach is to plan your schedule and determine when you'll be online and when you need to automate your posts.

Your turn! Plan ahead by evaluating these questions:

Are you manually sharing your content through your social media accounts?

Have you ever considered using a scheduling tool to help with this?

What tool(s) do you recommend for others to try and why?

5. Publish high-quality content

If you have an active personal brand and you want to maintain its standing, don't lose your momentum. You have to create fresh and compelling content using various social media, and this can include a blog, social media platforms and anything you can utilize to present your ideas to the world. However, you have to be careful. People are looking for high-quality content, and publishing numerous insignificant content for the sake of publishing won't get you very far.

Recommendations:

Don't publish sub-par content. If you're not happy with the quality of your work, people will notice that. Have friends, peers and mentors give a critique early on about your topic and approach. Don't wait until you've finished a draft to ask for opinions. Be consistent and publish as often as you can but yes it should be high-quality content. Don't worry about the output rate, and just focus on quality.

Your turn! Review your methods:

Do you ever ask other people to critique your work before publishing it?

What do you do to ensure you're publishing high-quality content?

What's more important to you quantity or quality?

11

LESSONS TO LEARN FROM PM NARENDRA MODI

Being Indian and being from personal branding field it will be an injustice to the book if I won't write about PM Narendra Modi, after all, there is so much to learn from Modi when it comes personal branding.

I don't know if you love Modi or you hate him, but I guarantee you can't avoid him because when it comes to personal brand and personal branding he definitely is the best and you can't ignore this fact. So, no matter who you are and which party or nation you belong to, you definitely have something to learn from Modi.

WHO IS NARENDRA MODI

Narendra Modi is an Indian politician who is serving as the current and 15th Prime Minister of India since 2014. Before he became Prime Minister, he had served many years as Chief Minister of Gujarat and had created a high rate of growth of GDP in Gujarat. He was always focused on development and change, and always asserted that he could concentrate on specific policies and bring about positive progress in a short amount of time. He won the support of the younger generation across India and the middle-class citizens. He received criticism for his role in the Gujarat Riots of 2002 but through his positive ideology and commitment to development he was able to shift the negative focus and project only good messages about himself, in effect giving himself a good quality personal brand and teaching us that even if your personal brand has been criticized, you can still work hard to restore your reputation.

Modi was sworn in as the Prime Minister on 26 May 2014 and began by liberalizing India's foreign direct investment policies enhancing foreign investment and opening barriers to allow for more flexibility and change within the business aspects of the country. He saw India and his personality as his own personal brand and developed it as any business would when improving and selling their personal brand, by focusing on the customer, the people of India, and trying to install a good deal for every person "Sabka Sath Sabka Vikas" means together with all, development for all - that's a concept, a vision he believes.

MAKE IN INDIA

In September 2014, Modi introduced an initiative called Make In India, which encouraged foreign companies to manufacture their products in India, and therefore providing more jobs and workflow for the people of India. He wanted to turn the country into a global manufacturing hub and so far, the country is still doing incredibly well in terms of how much we are producing for many other countries. As the reputation of good quality production grew, the demand by foreign companies also grew and the jobs availability for the people of India was growing overnight. This severely positively impacted the India market and Modi's initiative paid off, receiving many great reviews and much support from people of all ages and backgrounds.

POPULARITY

There is no other Prime Minister that has been followed as closely and watched as intensely as Narendra Modi. Many people have a lot of interest in him and are desperate to find out his next development plans for India and relationships with other nations, whilst others are waiting for him to make a mistake and fall. He is ranked among top 3 world leaders and to achieve such status in just a few years is an unbelievable achievement. Modi visited the USA and it was one of the most popular visits to be observed within the history of US politics, with billions of people wanted to hear and see the outcome of such visit and his collaborations with USA leader Donald Trump. Some people may have seen this as a regular visit and meeting between two of the world's most well-known Prime Ministers, but they could not be more mistaken, this visit was one of the strongest personal branding exercises ever seen within the field of politics. Read on further to understand more how Modi severely boosted his own personal brand image during his visit to the USA.

MODI AND PERSONAL BRANDING

There are various reasons why Narendra Modi can teach us many lessons and influence us to such a great extent. Throughout his position as the Prime Minister of India, he has done many great things, brought about many positive changes and also displayed himself in many wonderful lights, which in essence has boosted his personal brand and brand India. He has treated his role as if it was a personal business brand and he has marketed himself to appeal to and meet the needs of the customers, or in other words, the people of India, and their relations. He focuses on how best to reach his target market and how he can satisfy the desires of those around him and he creates strategies that will make for a better life for so many people, whilst bringing in new custom from abroad and retaining those great relationships for the purpose of security, stability and more positive development and growth for his country and people. Take a look below for some lessons that we can learn from Narendra Modi in relation to personal branding.

1. The USA Hype

Narendra Modi knew that as time has passed, India is becoming more and more westernized, and has adopted many cultures and habits that stem from the west. Many of India's people are based in these western countries for work, and some are choosing to reside there as they like the lifestyle. Despite having strong Hindu religious believes, Modi never oppose this change or transition for his country and rather he decided to educate himself better on the western culture so that he could relate more to his own people. This is why he chose to take a visit to the USA and soak up the culture whilst discussing the habits and ways of the country with their leader Donald Trump. This is important also concerning personal branding as it is vital to accept change, be malleable and take in to account the views and wishes of all those around you, this way your brand is not restricted to only your old-fashioned ways and can keep up with modern day development of the world.

2. The Way Modi Carries Himself

Modi has always been known as a confident man, and perhaps the most confident appearance was during his visit to the USA when he arrived dressed in his Indian Garb and was carrying his books from Shri Shri Ravi Shankar. He knew that he is representing brand India and that is why he carried with him the values and culture of the Indian people. He did not just follow the crowd or aim to fit in with the Americans, he differentiated and wanted to always be himself. This is an important lesson for any brand, don't follow the crowd, be yourself, maintain that individuality and stand out from all the followers. He was making a loud statement and one that future politicians will definitely take note of, in terms of representing their country and standing by their values. He showed true belief in himself. Modi was able to do this through thorough preparation, another great lesson for anybody who is considering personal branding, as rushed work will be failed work, so it is always important to be prepared and think carefully about the presentation of oneself.

3. Narendra Modi Spoke in Hindi

Modi chose to speak for at least half an hour within the UN Summit in his cultural language of Hindi, and this was perhaps the strongest statement he made when projecting himself on to the people and leaders of the world. This was a true moment of pride for the people of India, whether they live in India or abroad, this was a real proud time for them. Modi was fully able to speak in English, but he wanted to assert that despite travelling to other countries and considering the culture, he was proud of his own country and stood by them no matter what. His first priority was his own people, and this is a lesson that should be learned by other countries leaders, whose views often stray from the benefit and alliance with their own countrymen. He showed billions of people how a considerate and committed Prime Minister should behave. This can teach us a thing or two about personal branding, namely do not give up on your brand or become two entwined in what other brands are doing, focus on yourself and your own growth and don't try to be the same as others, be proud of what your brand is and project it in the way that you want to, without changing your image too much just to fit in with others. Maintain solidarity and belief in your personal branding strategy.

4. The "Make In India" Campaign

Just before heading over to the USA, Modi introduced the initiative of Make In India, whereby he as putting a lot of encouragement, thought and resources into opening up the channels between India and other countries for the purpose of manufacturing goods. He was hoping for various countries to relocate their production to India, offering lower production costs for the companies involved, whilst also generating a lot of work for the people of India. By doing this he was showing us that with careful consideration and thought, we can help everybody involved by just one thought or idea. This is an ideal principle when it comes to personal branding as it shows that you are aware of everybody involved and want to ensure that everybody is affected positively. It was also good that he has introduced this just before visiting the USA as it gave him the ideal chance to promote and make others aware of his new idea, maximizing the coverage of his personal brand idea for marketing purposes and generating interest and enquiries into the scheme.

5. The Reaction of the USA to Modi's Visit

Madison Square Garden was completely filled to listen to the speech of Narendra Modi. Many politics-based visits have been smaller scale and generate less interest amongst Americans, however, everybody wanted to be involved when Narendra Modi visited the USA. Indians and Americans alike all gathered together as one to listen to what he had to say and to learn as much as they could from him. He is now known as one of the strongest and most positive influencers in history regarding world country leaders and this showed by the popularity his visit received. Americans welcomed him with open arms and felt privileged to have him in their country sharing their culture and speaking so openly about himself and his own country. In terms of branding this is a lesson to be learned relating to how we affect others and make others feel. By making others feel safe, secure and interested, we can generate popularity and therefore create a great brand image.

6. Motivational Speaking

Modi used his visit to project on to the people of the world his beliefs that great things can be done if we all join hands and work together for the greater good of everybody. He displayed many principles of Martin Luther King Jr who was another adored and respected leader. Modi showed true passion and it was obvious to everybody that this was not scripted but straight from his heart. He promoted democracy and freedom and spoke passionately about the future of Indian youth and the youth of other countries, putting the statement that he wanted the younger generations to experience a better life. Relating to personal branding, passion is everything and without believing in yourself you cannot expect others to believe in you.

Listed below are the top qualities of Narendra Modi that set his personal brand apart and make him high-performance leader, rather than just leader:

Speaking Skills

Narendra Modi has terrific speaking skills, and his voice makes your head turn. Being a great speaker is a crucial skill for the powerful personal brand, the good speaking ability is something that will make you stand out from the crowd and get your message across.

Branding Fundamentals

Modi was remarkably clear in practicing the most powerful fundamental principles of branding: "Be different and Solve the Problem!". And must have noticed Modi has used these both fundamental principles very actively "Acche Din Aane Wale Hain" means Goods days are coming and "Sabka Sath Sabka Vikas" means Together with all, Development for all. By using these two taglines in his all the campaigns, he addressed the various issues close to public and assured them that their problems would be solved.

Likewise, create your USP and offer the solution, and you will see that this approach will differentiate you from the others.

Determination

Modi's defining characteristic is determination and an absolute commitment to success, he is determined to make it big for himself and for his country India. And this is something strong leaders have in common. It is often said that determination is the key to success so if you truly want to succeed in building your personal brand you must be determined because this fuels your motivation and will keep you moving forward.

Discipline

Modi has always led a disciplined life. Ever since he joined RSS as a Swayam Sevak, he has followed a disciplined regimen. He is the man who wakes up on time, sleeps on time and most importantly practices Yoga every single day. No personal success, achievement, or goal, can be achieved without self-discipline.

Fitness

No matter how busy Modi is but something he never forgets to practice every single day is Yoga. This love for Yoga is his main source of Modi's energy.

Numerous studies have defined the relationship between exercise and productivity, studies have discovered a positive correlation between regular exercise and improved productivity. So, no matter what you do and how old you are, keep health and wellness a priority.

Knowledgeable

My personal favorite characteristic of Modi is that he always keeps himself informed, every time you hear his speech anywhere and everywhere you will notice he appears knowledgeable and well informed. This quality makes him sound confident, well connected and friendly and you know this how great speaker connect with their audience.

In conclusion, Modi taught us a lot about personal branding, and instilled in us that how we carry ourselves says so much about who we are. Modi's personal brand has seen an incredible boost since taking the opportunity to share his passion in the USA and this can be a lesson to anybody regarding branding, that belief in yourself is the true key to success.

SUMMARY

The Concept of Personal Branding

It was in the late nineties that the concept of personal branding showed its capacity for influencing, inspiring, and empowering people. Nonetheless, it was only in recent years that this concept became more popular with the help of the internet. Today, a person who is determined to establish a successful personal brand can do it in the comforts of his own home. He can transform his life through a powerful personal brand.

Personal branding incorporates several key concepts including self-discovery, exploring passions, searching for a purpose, and pursuing goals which are consistent to the brand promise that you have created. You have to assess your current life and unite your authentic self to a personal brand that encapsulates your reputation, your credibility, and your unique offering to your target audience.

Communication Tools

Several tools are used for communication today, and they can range from the most personal, professional to global. It really depends on what is necessary for a given situation.

Personal branding veers away from the superficial and highlights the core values that people find more important in life. The communication tools that we utilize have become much more sophisticated to cater to the essential areas where we can find meaning and purpose.

Personal Image

You may have a perfect image, but it may not translate to your professional objective. First impressions last and you have to exert effort in how you look, too. Be presentable and charming to engage people in an exciting conversation. Establish good rapport in professional and personal relationships all the time.

Contemporary Documents

Until recently, a professional only used one or two personal marketing tools. I am referring to the resume and the cover letter. They are traditional, still relevant, but there are other more effective means to get noticed these days.

Now, you must begin to position your personal brand using other means with which you can show your value and not just tell it. Create brochures, short e-books, or reports wherein you can offer information about your work, your projects, and your achievements. If you bring something interesting and valuable, you can reach a wider audience.

Social Events

All the tools of communication and personal marketing are only means to get that direct contact. The business meals or those talks over coffee are essential to building rapport, secure confidence, and strengthen professional bonds.

In your personal brand strategy, you must allocate time to re-establish your bond with your customers and stakeholders by updating them on current activities. You must be aware of the presentations, conferences, events, fairs, or any other type of social or professional meetings in which you can contact those who can help you or give you excellent advice.

Meetings

Work meetings, screening interviews, or annual evaluation are face-to-face meetings where you can introduce your personal brand. Take advantage of these great opportunities to share your ideas. You should consider such encounters with one or more people as an opportunity to position yourself and sell what you do.

Blog or Website

A blog or website is a must. To promote your personal brand, you must have a website of your own, managed and controlled by you, where you can showcase your work. It is not about having constant activity and contributing content every day; you just need to put compelling content – quality over quantity. What I recommend is that you have the virtual portfolio that you can link to those who are interested in your work anytime.

Conferences

Other tools of communication for your personal brand are the courses, seminars, workshops and conferences that you can organize or join. Create the opportunity to address a group of people who are willing to listen to you about something you are passionate about and something that will benefit their lives.

Social media networks

Making good use of social media networks can propel your growth in personal branding. This method requires careful planning of all your posts and shares because you carry your brand image with every click of the mouse. Post responsibly. When choosing a platform, you should keep in mind that there are professional social networks like LinkedIn that are worth spending more time on. Facebook and Instagram is a great platform as long as you use it wisely.

Virtual presentations

One of the goals of personal branding is to build credibility for yourself or your business. If you want to get it, you must offer some proof. Therefore, you must use all the means at your disposal to teach, show, and demonstrate your value. For example, if you are a consultant or an expert in a certain field, you can create a presentation and upload it to a site like Slideshare or Udemy.

Books or E-books

It used to be difficult to publish a book – too expensive and ineffective. Today, you can write, publish, and even sell an ebook by following simple steps online. Like everything worth your while, a book requires effort and time but having published one puts you in a position where you can be viewed as a person of authority in your field thus, you can be trusted and respected. From a personal branding standpoint, it is one of the most valuable tools to use for boosting your credibility and enhancing your reputation.

If you won't build your brand someone will hire you to help build theirs.

So, Start Building Your Personal Brand Today!

9 789353 113629

Printed at Repro India Ltd.